Instant
Expert

BIKE
by
Paul Mason

MECHANIC

CAPSTONE PRESS
a capstone imprint

Velocity is published by
Capstone Press, a Capstone imprint,
151 Good Counsel Drive, P.O. Box 669,
Mankato, Minnesota 56002.

www.capstonepub.com

First published 2011
Copyright © 2011 A & C Black
Publishers Limited

Original concept: Paul Mason
Project management: Paul Mason
Design: Mayer Media

032011
006117ACF11

Library of Congress Cataloging-in-Publication
Data

Mason, Paul, 1967-
  Bike mechanic : how to be an ace bike
mechanic / by Paul Mason.
    p. cm. -- (Instant expert)
  Includes bibliographical references and index.
  ISBN 978-1-4296-6882-8 (library binding)
  1. Bicycles--Maintenance and repair--Juvenile
literature. I. Title.
  TL430.M37 2012
  629.28'772--dc22
                                    2011010222

WARNING!
**Some of the techniques described in
this book are dangerous, or can lead
to dangerous situations if performed
incorrectly. Only undertake them when you
are 100% confident you can do so safely.**

This book is produced using paper made from
wood grown in managed, sustainable forests.
It is natural, renewable, and recyclable. The
logging and manufacturing processes conform
to the environmental regulations of the
country of origin.

Photo acknowledgements
All interior photos Paul Mason, except: p.10
top, original patent application; p.10 middle
Nyíro András; p.10 bottom, detail from original
advertisement; p.11 top, original advertisement;
p.11 bottom, original advertisement; p.27/45 Hu
Totya; p.41 bottom, Bram Souffreau.

Cover photos © Shutterstock

Contents

Why become an
expert mechanic?

Ever ridden along with the gears on your bike going 'rackety-clack, rackety-clack', every time you turn the pedals? Or stood at the side of the road scratching your head, looking at a flat tire and wondering what to do? Or wondered how to keep your brakes from screeching? Then this book is for you.

HELP YOUR FRIENDS
Not only will you find out how to get *your* bicycle running as smoothly as a python slithering across a sheet of glass. You'll also be able to step in *just* as your friends are about to give up, point out exactly what they're doing wrong, and show them how to put the problem right. How satisfying is that?

FINDING THE RIGHT INFO
At the back of the book there's a **troubleshooting** section to help you diagnose the particular sickness your machine is suffering from. Clicking noise when you pedal? Jumping gears? Keep slipping forwards on your seat? **Troubleshooting** tells you where to look for a fix. Or, if you know where the problem lies (handlebars, bottom bracket, etc.), just use the contents page or index to go straight to the relevant place.

FYI!
These features are scattered throughout the book. They contain information you can casually drop into conversation to amaze, astound, and impress your friends.

Whip off that tire in seconds - even if you don't have tire levers! See page 33 to find out how.

Whatever kind of bike you (or your friends) ride, you can probably make it run better using the tips in this book.

SPECIAL TOOLS
The tools you need for most jobs are listed on pages 6 and 7. Some jobs also require specialist tools, which are listed in features like this one.

LOST FOR WORDS
Look here for explanations of those tricky, technical words.

SAVE CASH
Every time you go into a bike shop to get your bike fixed, it costs money. With a few simple tools, most jobs can be done at home - saving you a lot of cash to spend on new bike equipment.

SECRET TRICK
Look out for the **Secret Trick** features that'll give you extra information, including handy hints and tips on the techniques featured. Use the step by step photos to help you perfect each one.

Types of bikes

Years ago, almost every bike had one gear, very simple brakes, a rigid frame, and similar seats, handlebars and other parts. With such simple parts, it must have been very easy to be a bike mechanic. Today, there are so many different types of bikes that things are a lot more complicated. Even just naming the parts is a tricky job!

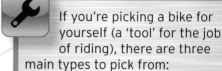

If you're picking a bike for yourself (a 'tool' for the job of riding), there are three main types to pick from:
• **Road bikes, with smooth tires**
• **Mountain bikes, with knobby tires for off-road grip**
• **Crossover bikes, which combine some features of both**

SINGLE-SPEED BIKES

Single-speed bikes are today's closest equivalent to simple, old-fashioned machines. They have only one gear, so the only **drivetrain** issue for a mechanic is to make sure the chain is tight enough and the rear wheel properly aligned in the frame. Single-speeds are ridden either 'free', which means you can stop pedalling whenever you want, or 'fixed', which means you have to keep pedalling whenever the wheels are spinning.

BIKES WITH GEARS

Most modern bikes have gears – usually anything from 18 to 30. For many people, how a bike's gears work is a complete mystery. Almost nothing wins you more respect from non-mechanics than crouching down and adjusting someone's gears so that they run perfectly.

cranks metal arms that join the pedals to the bike
drivetrain parts that let the rider power the bike along
rigid frame a bike frame that does not have any kind of shock absorbers

a disc brake

BRAKES

There are two basic kinds of brakes: rim brakes, which work by clamping down on the wheel rim, and disc brakes, which clamp down on a metal disc attached to the wheel hub. Rim brakes are fitted to road and general-purpose bikes, as well as some mountain bikes. Disc brakes are more of a specialty, and are usually fitted to serious off-road bikes.

SUSPENSION

Most modern mountain bikes come with suspension at one or both ends. Working on suspensions is a specialist job, and requires unusual tools. It's best left to a bike shop, rather than working on it yourself.

SECRET TRICK

When you're picking a new bike, it's important to buy one with a frame that fits you. Here are two quick ways to check this:

1 With your feet flat on the floor, measure the gap between the top tube and your crotch. With a sloping top tube, a gap of 7.5cm/3in is about right. With a straight-across top tube, leave about 2.5cm/1in.

2 Set the seat to the right height (see pages 14-15), then sit on the bike with the **cranks** parallel to the ground. Press your knees together: on bikes with a sloping top tube, they should meet above the top tube.

FYI!
Early Tour de France riders were forbidden to accept help.

Tools and rules for happy mechanics

If you've ever tried to chop off a tree branch using a pocket knife, you'll know that every job is easier with the right tools. It's the same for bike mechanics. With the wrong tools, parts get damaged and knuckles get skinned. With the right tools, the job is faster and easier.

BASIC TOOLS

Today, cycle parts are much more standardized than ever before. Incredibly, it's possible to put together a whole bike with just a pocket multi-tool and a set of cable cutters. But it's a good idea to have a few more items in your toolbox than that. Most of the jobs shown in this book can be done using the tools shown below:

Almost every basic maintenance job can be done with just a decent multi-tool. Because they're small, multi-tools are not as good as proper tools – but in an emergency, a multi-tool usually gets the job done.

Long-handled allen keys are the most useful tools for working on a bike. Almost all the bolts and fasteners on a modern bike have allen-key sockets.

For some jobs, usually to do with the drivetrain, you need a medium-sized adjustable wrench or a set of spanners of different sizes.

It's worthwhile getting a couple of holders for your tools to keep them dry and in good condition:
- **A toolbox with spaces to store small parts**
- **A seatbag for carrying tools on the bike**

WORK CLEAN

'Work clean' is a good rule for bike mechanics. This means keeping yourself, the bike, and all the tools and parts you use as clean as possible. Keep a bag of old rags handy whenever you work on a bike, and use them to clean any parts you remove. Clean out the **threads** of all bolts, then rub in some fresh bike grease before reinstalling them.

FYI!

The first bike mechanics were usually village blacksmiths. Their tools included a hammer, anvil, and forge. Imagine having to fit those in your tool kit.

multi-tool bike tool with several different functions
thread spiral line cut into the length of a bolt or screw

SECRET TRICK

Whenever you take apart anything on a bike, use these tips to help you remember how they should go back together again:

1 Have a big sheet of newspaper lying nearby. On it, lay out parts in the order you've taken them apart or off the bike. That way, you'll know the order they go back on.

2 If a job is particularly complicated, take photos of each stage (including before you start work) with a digital camera. They'll remind you of what it's meant to look like once you've put it all back together again.

Birth of the bicycle

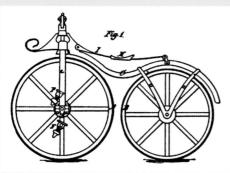

This drawing was a plan for the first pedal-driven bicycle in 1866.

Surprisingly, bicycles haven't existed for all that long. The first bikes looked quite similar to today's, but they didn't have pedals.

In England 'regular' bikes like this became known as 'penny farthings'.

THE RUNNING MACHINE

The first known bikes of the early 1800s were the German *laufmaschine*. *Laufmaschine* is German for 'running machine', and these bikes had no pedals or gears. You moved them by sitting on the seat and running along, like the **balance bikes** young children use today. Thousands of *laufmaschine* were built. People used them as an alternative to traveling by horse.

PEDALS AND THE 'REGULAR' BIKE

The next big step in bike design was to add pedals. At first, these were fixed to the front wheel. This meant that one turn of the pedals equalled one turn of the wheels. On flat ground, people were able to ride faster than they could have pushed a *laufmaschine*. To go even quicker, they added bigger wheels. A bigger wheel would travel further in one turn of the pedals than a small one. Eventually these bikes, called 'regulars', had giant front wheels and very small back ones.

balance bike small bike with no pedals often used by young children

bloomers an early kind of trouser for women, baggy at the top and ending gathered at the knee

APPEARANCE OF THE MODERN BIKE

Around 1900, bicycles with chain-driven rear wheels began to appear. This made it possible to have wheels the same size, which made the bike much easier and safer to ride. This kind of bike became known as a 'safety' cycle. Safety cycles became wildly popular. They are recognizably the same kind of machine as people ride today.

SECRET HISTORY

From about 1900, safety cycles rapidly became extremely popular – especially with women. For the first time, women were easily able to travel under their own power, leading the American writer Susan B. Anthony to call bicycles "freedom machines."

At the time, almost all women wore long skirts, which were impossible to cycle in. The biking craze led to new clothes called "rational clothing" being developed.

"Rational clothing" included **bloomers**. Wearing these, women were able to do much more physical activity than in the past. Bicycles soon became a symbol of women's freedom.

Woman wearing trousers on magazine cover from the early 1900s

FYI!

On a 'regular' bike, a bigger front wheel was faster. Wheel sizes were measured in inches. Today, expert mechanics still describe the size and potential speed of bike gears in "gear inches."

11

Bike cleaning

Any mechanic will tell you that before you start working on a bike, it needs to be clean. Otherwise grease and dirt get on your fingers and hands, and from there they spread to your face, hair, and clothes.

To do a great job of cleaning a bike before working on it, you need:
- **Soft sponge and brushes**
- **Bike or car wash soap**

Start by turning the bike upside down and resting it on its seat and handlebars. This is the easiest way to clean underneath the bike. (Wrap the seat before turning the bike upside down.)

Next use a soft brush to clean dirt from around the brakes and levers. It's OK to use warm water and bike wash for this job, but don't use degreaser. If you get degreaser on the brake rims, they will make a terrible shrieking noise next time you try to slow down.

seatpost tube that connects the seat to the bike frame

Keep the seat dry while cleaning the bike by wrapping it in an old plastic bag and sealing it. This is especially important if it's made of leather.

Also brush off the pedals and cranks (again, it's good to use warm water and bike wash) to get rid of big bits of dirt. You might have to dig out stubborn bits of dirt and mud, but do it gently or the bike could be damaged.

1 Cover the seat with an old plastic bag. Make sure the bag doesn't have any little holes in it.

2 Seal the bag against the **seatpost** using a zip tie, rubber band, or piece of string.

Once everything else has been cleaned, wash the main tubes down with a soft sponge. Finally, rinse with cold water and dry the bike.

3 Once the bike is dry, remove the bag. Leather seats should be cleaned once in a while with special leather polish, or wiped clean with a damp cloth.

There are separate instructions for cleaning the drivetrain, which is a bit more complicated, on page 22.

FYI!

Never use dishwashing liquid to clean a bike. It usually contains salt, and will corrode the metal parts.

Are you **sitting comfortably?**

One of the best adjustments you can make to a bike, whether it's yours or a friend's, is to the seat height. If the seat's too low or too high, the rider won't be able to get enough power into the pedals and will be uncomfortable. Everyone has a different amount of flexibility, so not everyone the same size needs the same seat height.

FINDING A ROUGH SEAT HEIGHT
If you are in a hurry, this technique is a good way to get your seat at roughly the correct height. Find somewhere that you can sit on the bike and lean safely against a wall. Put your heels on the pedals. With the pedal as far down as it will go, your leg should be not quite at full stretch, with a very slight bend in your knee. If your leg is at full stretch, or you have to move your hips to reach the pedal, the seat is a bit too high. Lower it 2.5cm/1in and try again. The bike should now be comfortable to ride.

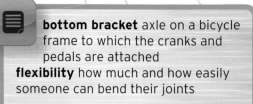

bottom bracket axle on a bicycle frame to which the cranks and pedals are attached
flexibility how much and how easily someone can bend their joints

FYI!
Five-time Tour de France winner Eddy Merckx, who was fanatical about how his bike was set up, always used to set his seat absolutely level. So did seven-time Tour winner Lance Armstrong.

The extra tools you need for this job can be found in most homes:
- **Tape measure**
- **Calculator**
- **Bubble level**

FINDING AN EXACT SEAT HEIGHT – STEP 1
This technique is mainly used by racing cyclists, but works just as well for everyone else. Measure your inside leg. Stand against a wall, with a hardback book between your legs. Position the book so that it is in the same position as a bicycle seat would be. Get a friend to hold the book in place as you step away from it, then measure the distance from the floor to the top of the book.

FINDING AN EXACT SEAT HEIGHT – STEP 2
Multiply your inside-leg measurement by 0.88. This tells you the height to set your seat, measured from the middle of the **bottom bracket** to the top of the seat. Measure in a straight line, in line with the bike's seat tube. Once the seat is at the correct height, lightly tighten up the seatpost clamp, then make sure the seat is pointing straight forwards. Now completely tighten the seatpost clamp. This needs to be done up tight, or the seatpost will slip down inside the frame.

SECRET TRICK
Bike seats are usually most comfortable when they are set absolutely level, or perhaps very slightly tilted backwards:

1 Rest the bike on completely level ground. Loosen the seat-clamp bolt so that the seat can be tilted back and forth.

2 Rest a spirit level along the seat, and adjust the seat so that the bubble is centered.

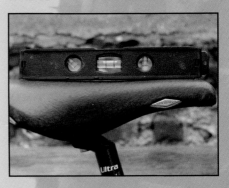

3 Tighten the seat-clamp bolt and re-check. Sometimes tightening affects the angle of the seat.

Set up and adjust brakes

There are few things more painful to a mechanic than badly set up brakes. Not only do they fail to stop the bike, they also lead to the rider rolling to a stop with the brakes making a terrible noise.

Adjusting 'brake feel' can usually be done using just your fingers. To set up the pads you might find it useful to have:

• **a third-hand tool**

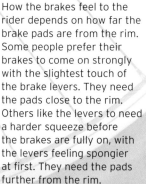

TYPES OF RIM BRAKES
Most bikes are fitted with rim brakes, which work by clamping down on the wheel rim. The two main kinds are V-brakes, which are usually fitted to all-purpose and some mountain bikes, and cantilever brakes, which are fitted to road bikes. Both work on the same principle, and can be adjusted in similar ways.

SETTING BRAKE FEEL
How the brakes feel to the rider depends on how far the brake pads are from the rim. Some people prefer their brakes to come on strongly with the slightest touch of the brake levers. They need the pads close to the rim. Others like the levers to need a harder squeeze before the brakes are fully on, with the levers feeling spongier at first. They need the pads further from the rim.

ADJUSTING FEEL
The distance of the pads from the rim, and therefore the feel of the brakes, is controlled by the length of the brake cable. You can adjust this in several ways, but the simplest is to use an adjustment **knurl** on the brake lever (for V-brakes) or the brake itself (for cantilever brakes). Undoing this knurl will pull the brake pads closer to the rim. Screwing it in will move the brake pads further away from the rim. Make these adjustments in half turns of the knurl, until you find a setting that feels right.

third-hand tool special clamp used by mechanics to hold parts in place while they work on them

knurl knob with a ridged surface, which makes it easier to grip

SET EQUAL DISTANCE

When the brakes are pulled on, the brake pads should hit the rim at the same time. All brakes have a screw or allen bolt that allows you to adjust this. Screwing it in will move the pad further from the rim, screwing out will do the opposite. Make these adjustments in small steps because they are quite sensitive.

FYI!

Early bikes didn't have any brakes at all. If you wanted to stop, you had to pedal more slowly – or jump off!

SECRET TRICK

The main reason for a bike having squeaky brakes is that the pads aren't lined up properly:

1 Look at the pads from in front or behind. Do they hit the rims at the same place and angle?

2 Now look at the pads. Are they lined up with the rim?

3 If the pads need adjustment, loosen the allen bolt that holds them in place, hold the brake against the rim with your hand, and move the pad into the correct position. Hold it clamped in place and tighten the allen bolt.

Fitting new
disc-brake pads

This is a relatively simple job, and can be done without specialist tools:
- **Repair stand**
- **Cloth**
- **Cleaning fluid**

Disc brakes are now available on all but the cheapest mountain bikes, and some road bikes. They are heavier than rim brakes, but offer much more powerful stopping performance. As the pads wear out, they need to be replaced. These instructions are for Shimano, the most common disc brakes.

REMOVE THE OLD PADS
Clamp the bike into the repair stand, and remove the wheels. Pull off the metal clip that holds the pad fixing bolt in place, then unscrew the bolt itself.

Next remove the pads from the brake body. Some pads pull out, away from the wheel hub. Others have tabs to pull them towards the hub. Make a careful note of how the pads fit together.

CLEAN THE PISTON AND CALIPER
Removing the pad will reveal the **pistons** that sit underneath the pad. If the pistons (the circular shapes at the center of the brake) are sticking out, use a plastic tire lever to push them back flat with the body of the brake. Next clean the area around the pistons.

piston metal cylinder that slides in and out of its housing

SECRET TRICK

Most bike wheels fasten up using a quick-release skewer. To take the wheel out of the frame and forks, you simply flip open the lever and turn it around a few times while holding the nut on the other side.

1 If possible, always do the levers up so that they are pointing backwards. This makes it less likely they will get caught in something and accidentally flip open.

2 If they cannot be pointed backwards, always make sure the quick-release levers are tucked in and as far out of the way as possible.

REPLACE PADS

Fit the new pads into the holding clip. Then put them into the brake. Line up the holes with the holes for the pad fixing bolt, then reinstall this. Put the wheel back on the bike, and test the working of the brake.

FYI!

One big advantage of disc brakes for an off-road bike is that they don't get clogged up with mud like rim brakes do.

Adjusting **gears** and **chains**

Most bikes have gear systems that use a derailleur **and** freewheel **to give the rider a choice of pedalling speeds. Easy gears let you cruise uphill. Hard gears allow you to speed downwards, leaning into corners like a dirt-bike racer. And the in-between gears are for in-between terrain. But none of them do you any good if they don't work properly.**

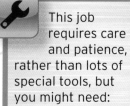

This job requires care and patience, rather than lots of special tools, but you might need:
• **Small screwdriver (either flat or Philips head)**

SKIPPING AND MISSING GEARS

The most common problem with a bike's gears is that they are not properly aligned. This causes the bike to make *ka-churr* noises whenever the rider tries to change gear, before it eventually settles down. To sort this out, you need to turn the bike upside down, and make adjustments to the **derailleur**.

ADJUSTING THE DERAILLEUR

Put the bike into its bottom gear (the smallest **cog** on the **freewheel**). Screw in the adjuster at the back of the derailleur, where the gear cable goes into the derailleur, as far as possible. Then try to shift into second gear. Turn the bike's pedals slowly. You will probably find the bike stays in first gear.

MOVING UP A GEAR

Keep turning the bike's pedals, and start unscrewing the adjuster as you pedal. Eventually the chain will start to jump. Keep pedalling and unscrewing, and finally the bike will jump into second gear. Unscrew the adjuster another half turn so that the chain is running smoothly on the cog.

cog toothed disc that fits into a bike's chain and grips it
derailleur hinged arm that allows the bike to change gear
freewheel cluster of cogs attached to the bike's rear wheel

SECRET TRICK

If your gears won't shift properly even after adjusting the derailleur, check two more things:

1 Make sure the derailleur is hanging down straight. If not, you'll need to take it to a bike shop to be pulled back – this is a specialist job.

2 If the derailleur is straight, adjust the limit screws. The 'H' screw controls how far away from the wheel the derailleur and chain can go. The 'L' screw controls how far in the derailleur and chain can come.

CHECK YOUR WORK

Now use the gear lever to run up and down the gears a couple of times. The gears should shift smoothly from one cog to the next in both directions. If they are slow shifting down, screw the adjuster in a quarter turn at a time until they run smoothly. If they are slow shifting up, screw the adjuster out a quarter turn at a time.

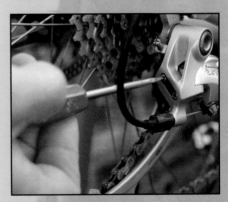

Cleaning chains
and **gears**

If you keep just one part of your bike clean, make it the drivetrain (the chain, freewheel and chainset). A well-looked-after drivetrain will work smoothly and last for years. A badly maintained one may only last a few months and make a nasty squeaking noise every time you push on the pedals.

This job does require special tools:
- **Chain bath and cleaning fluid**
- **Stiff brush**
- **Clean rags**
- **Chain oil**

FYI!
Not all bikes use chains to power the rear wheel. Recently, some bikes have been fitted with belt drives instead.

CLEAN THE FREEWHEEL, DERAILLEUR AND CHAINSET
Put a little cleaning fluid in a small pot, then dip your stiff brush in it. Scrub clean the freewheel and derailleur **jockey wheels**. Rinse the brush in the fluid as soon as it gets dirty, or you'll just be spreading dirt and oil around. The lazy way to do this is by holding the brush still and turning the cranks, but watch out for the brush getting caught in the chain teeth. Scrub the chainset too.

chainset the cranks and chainrings which are attached to a bike's bottom bracket
jockey wheel small, toothed wheel inside the derailleur arm

GIVE YOUR CHAIN A BATH

Now use the chain bath on the chain. These work differently, but they all have an upper reservoir that you fill with cleaning fluid before clipping the upper and lower parts over the chain. Now run the chain through the bath while turning the cranks and pushing the button that releases cleaning fluid onto the chain. Turn the cranks so that the whole chain runs through the bath at least three times.

CLEAN AND DRY

Tip the dirty cleaning fluid down the drain (always use environmentally friendly cleaning fluid, which will not harm the environment when it is disposed of). Then use a clean rag to wipe the whole drivetrain clear of cleaning fluid before letting it dry in the air for an hour or so. Everything should now be sparkly clean and ready to be oiled.

SECRET TRICK

The right amount of oil protects a bike's chain, makes it last longer, and makes it work well.

1 First, oil the outer edge of the chain, making sure a little oil gets on each link. The easiest way is to hold the oil container in one place, and slowly pedal the chain backwards with your hand.

2 Next, oil the inner edge of the chain, again making sure a little oil goes on each link.

3 Put oil on a clean cloth, and use it to wipe off any excess oil. Do this to all four sides of the chain. It spreads the oil around as well as clearing off excess.

Fitting a new chain

This can be a dirty job:
- **Latex gloves**
- **Chain splitter**

Bike chains have to bear heavy loads, and even a well-looked-after chain eventually wears out. The most obvious sign that a chain has worn is when the gears start to skip and slip, even though they're perfectly adjusted (see pages 20-21). When this happens, the chain needs to be replaced.

REMOVE THE OLD CHAIN

This is such a dirty job that it might be worth cleaning the old chain before you take it off. Otherwise, wear thin latex gloves to keep the oil off your hands and clothes. Some modern chains have a special link which you can push together to break the chain (circled). If not, you need to use a chain splitter to push a link pin out of the old chain. Remove the chain and put it in the metal recycling.

THREAD THE NEW CHAIN THROUGH

Once you have sized the new chain (see the Secret Trick on page 25 for information about doing this), thread it through the freewheel and derailleurs – don't forget to thread it through the front derailleur as well. Shift the front derailleur on to the smallest cog, and drape the chain over the **bottom bracket shell**.

bottom bracket shell part of a bike's frame that holds the bottom bracket

breakable link special section of chain used to join two ends by hand

fixing pin thin cylinder of metal designed to make joining two ends of a chain easier

JOIN THE NEW CHAIN TOGETHER

With the chain all threaded through, double check that everything is in the correct position. (Once the chain is joined together it's a bad idea to split it again.) Modern chains are usually fastened using either a special **breakable link** or a **fixing pin**. If the chain uses a link, you can join it by hand, simply by attaching the ends and pulling. With a fixing pin, you position the chain by hand, then use a chain tool to push the pin through, before breaking off the excess pin.

FYI!

In the 2010 Tour de France, Andy Schleck lost 39 seconds to his rival Alberto Contador when his chain slipped off. Contador eventually won—beating Schleck by 39 seconds.

SECRET TRICK

When you fit a new chain, it's important to get the chain length right. Too short and the bike may not shift gear properly; too long, and the chain may rub against the frame.

1 You can lay your old chain against the new one side by side, then use a chain tool to shorten the new chain to the same length as the old one.

2 Or, without threading it through the derailleur, put the chain around the biggest cogs on the front and rear. Add one link, and the chain should be the correct length.

Fixed wheels
and single speeds

Today, most road bikes have 18 or 20 gears. Mountain bikers disagree about whether it's better to have 20 or 30. But there's a small band of riders who don't take part in this debate, because they already know exactly how many gears they need: one.

SINGLE SPEED vs. FIXED

There are two kinds of one-geared bike: single speed and fixed. A single-speed bike is just like any other, apart from having only one gear. You can stop pedalling and **coast** along whenever you like. On a fixed-gear bike, though, you cannot stop pedalling if the back wheel is going around. Ride your normal bike and see how often you stop pedalling to go around corners or slow down – you'll see how different a fixed-wheel bike would be.

WHY ONLY ONE GEAR?

1) In winter, a bike with one gear is much easier to keep running clean and smoothly. There are no derailleurs, freewheels, chainsets, or gear levers and cables to look after.
2) Some riders feel it is easier to enjoy other aspects of biking when they are not constantly worrying about whether they are in the best gear.
3) Riding a fixed-wheel bike is often said to improve your pedalling technique, helping you pedal with what cyclists call **souplesse**.

Bike polo, using fixed-gear bikes on a
football court or a basketball court,
has become popular. Here Austria is
playing Hungary.

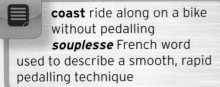

coast ride along on a bike
without pedalling
souplesse French word
used to describe a smooth, rapid
pedalling technique

FYI!

Henri Desgrange, the
founder of the Tour de
France: "I still feel that
variable gears are only for
people over forty-five. Isn't
it better to triumph by the
strength of your muscles
than by the artifice of a
derailleur? We are getting
soft... As for me, give me
a fixed gear!"

THE ULTIMATE CITY BIKE

Fixed-wheel bikes first became
popular with bike couriers working in
big cities such as San Francisco, New
York, London and Tokyo. The bikes
were cheap to buy, easy to fix, and
– unless you knew how to ride one
– hard to steal. It wasn't long before
other riders caught on to the fun of
riding fixed, or perhaps single-speed,
bikes. These machines have become
a common sight on the streets of
cities all around the world.

Servicing the **cranks**

The most common cause of a clicking bike – one that makes a ratchety clicking noise every time the pedals turn – is loose cranks. The cranks are put under pressure every time a rider pushes on the pedals. On a square-taper bottom bracket **they can easily work loose. Every mechanic needs to know how to remove, clean, and reassemble a bike's cranks.**

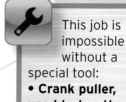

This job is impossible without a special tool:
• **Crank puller, used to tug the crank off the bike**

REMOVING THE CRANKS
First, remove the crank-bolt cover, which is usually attached with a large allen bolt. (The crank bolts on both sides undo counterclockwise.) These are usually tightly done up, so it takes a lot of force to free them. Once freed, they spin off very easily.

SCREW IN THE CRANK PULLER
This job should be done by hand, since that way you can feel if the puller is spinning easily into the crank. (See the Secret Trick on page 29 for advice about how to do this without damaging the crank's thread.) Screw out the rear part of the puller (the part that the mechanic in the photo is holding in his right hand) several turns. Now screw the front part of the puller into the crank.

REMOVE THE CRANK
Grip the rear part of the puller using an adjustable spanner. Hold the crank in your other hand to hold it steady, and screw the puller into the crank. It pushes against the bottom bracket, forcing the crank off. At first this will probably need a lot of force, but as soon as the crank is loose it will come off very quickly.

REMOVE OPPOSITE CRANK, CLEAN, AND REINSTALL

Do exactly the same on the other crank. You will be left with the bottom bracket **spindles** sticking out: wipe these surfaces clean with a rag, then use the rag to clean the holes in the cranks and the area around them. Apply a tiny bit of grease to the spindles, then push the cranks back on by hand. Screw in the crank-bolt cover, then tighten it up using a long-handled allen key. This pushes the crank back onto the spindle, so it needs to be done up tightly.

> **spindles** outer parts of the bottom bracket, to which the cranks are bolted
> **square-taper bottom bracket** most common type of bottom bracket, like the one shown in the photos above

SECRET TRICKS

When you're working on a bike it's important not to damage the threads of any parts by screwing them in at slightly the wrong angle.

1 One way to find an accurate angle for a thread is to try screwing it in *backwards*, in the opposite direction to the way it should go. At a certain point, you will hear or feel a little 'click'.

2 This is the sound of the two threads meeting, then dropping into place. Now turn the part in the correct direction. It should screw smoothly in.

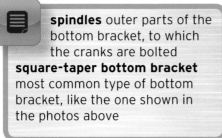

Bottom brackets

Like chains, bottom brackets suffer a lot of punishment. They sit low down, right next to the ground, in everything from dry-and-dusty to wet-and-muddy conditions. Through it all, they keep on turning sweetly – until one day, they don't. The bearings inside get rough and loose, and that's when you know it's time for a new bottom bracket.

> This job is impossible without a special tool:
> • **Bottom-bracket extractor**

CHECKING THE BOTTOM BRACKET
There's an easy test to see if the bottom bracket is worn out. Unhook the chain from the chainset and rest it on the bottom bracket shell so that the cranks can spin freely. Holding the seat tube in one hand, spin the cranks as hard as possible. If you can feel - or even hear - a grindy, grumbly sensation, the bottom bracket needs to be replaced.

BOTTOM BRACKET REMOVAL
First remove the cranks on both sides (see pages 28-29). Now insert the bottom-bracket tool into the bottom bracket. If one side is metal, always unscrew that one first. If not, unscrew the non-drive side first. Grip the bottom-bracket tool with an adjustable spanner - take care to hold the tool firmly in place, since it's easy to let it skid out.

LOOSENING DIRECTIONS
Most bottom brackets are threaded the same way on both sides. This means the non-drive side unscrews counterclockwise, but the drive side unscrews clockwise. A few bottom brackets are threaded so that both sides unscrew counterclockwise. These are often marked "36 x 24".

bearings short for 'ball bearings', tiny solid-metal balls that allow metal parts to move smoothly next to one another
burr raised, uneven piece of metal
drive side the side of the bike with the gears and chain on it (also sometimes called the right side)

INSTALL NEW BOTTOM BRACKET

Clean out the threads of the frame with a brass brush, then a clean rag. Grease them carefully, then screw in the main body of the new bottom bracket by hand. Once it is in as tightly as possible, screw it in as far as possible using the bottom-bracket tool and adjustable spanner. Next do the same on the other side, and reinstall the cranks.

SECRET TRICK

Sometimes, when the threads on the frame have become worn down, even tightly screwed– in bottom brackets feel a bit loose, or make a creaking or ticking noise. This trick sometimes sorts out the problem:

1 Clean the thread with a brass brush, which will remove any **burrs** of metal and deep dirt or grease.

2 Wrap the thread in plumber's tape, which you can get from most DIY stores. Press it into place with your thumb.

3 Screw the part back in. It should now feel nice and snug.

FYI!

Square-taper bottom brackets are the most common kind, but there are at least four others – and each requires different tools!

Tires, tubes and **punctures**

One of the first mechanic skills any rider learns is how to mend a puncture. Once you've taken the wheel off (see page 19 for information about this), you need to find the puncture, strip down the tire and inner tube, make a repair, and put it all back together again.

The repair patches are obviously essential, and this job is easier with:
• **Tire levers (strong plastic ones are best)**
• **Bicycle pump**
• **Repair patches**

STRIP THE TIRE AND INNER TUBE
Pull the tire off the rim on one side using a tire lever, starting on the opposite side of the wheel from the valve. Push the valve up through the hole in the rim, then pull out the whole inner tube. Lay the tube on top of the tire, with the valve right by the hole it just came out of.

FINDING THE PUNCTURE
Sit on the ground, and lay the wheel and tube across your legs. Pump up the tube, and listen for the hiss of escaping air to show you where the puncture is.

MAKE A REPAIR
Patch the hole using a pre-prepared adhesive patch. Blow the inner tube up a bit to make sure there aren't any more holes, and check the tire near the repair to see if objects such as thorns or glass are sticking through it (if so, remove them carefully to avoid splinters).

FYI!
Early bicycles were called 'boneshakers' – they had no tires, just strips of iron on wooden wheels!

bicycle pump hand-powered pump for inflating bicycle tires
valve part of a tire the pump attaches to

PUT IT ALL TOGETHER

Finally put everything back together. Put the valve back through its hole, then put the inner tube back inside the tire before fitting the tire back on to the rim. Start beside the valve, and work your way around to the opposite side.

SECRET TRICKS

You can usually get a tire off a wheel without tire levers, using just your thumbs:

1 Make sure the tire is fully deflated.

2 Starting by the valve, push the inside edge of the tire into the middle of the rim.

3 Steadily work your way around, using your left and right hands, until they meet opposite the valve.

4 The tire should now be loose enough to be levered off the rim using your thumbs. If not, repeat the process until it is.

Bicycle tourist

One of the great things about a bike is the freedom it gives you. As long as your bike is running well, you can go almost anywhere. It's amazing how far you can get in just a day. Or you can try overnight touring: some people spend weeks traveling around by bike.

WHAT TO TAKE

Whatever the weather, it pays to be prepared. It's always worth taking a pump, puncture-repair patches, a multi-tool, and water on a ride, and for longer distances most people take some extra clothing. As a minimum you should pack:

- waterproof jacket
- fleece vest
- hat
- money and cell phone in a waterproof bag
- snacks
- water

CARRYING KIT – DAY RIDES

How you carry your kit depends on how far you're going and what kind of bike you have. On a half-day ride in good weather, you can usually carry what you need in your pockets. For longer rides, backpacks can be uncomfortable, so riders fix a **rack** to their bike and use it to carry a little bundle of equipment. If your bike has mounting points, a rack can be fixed to a bike's frame. Otherwise, a seatpost-mounted rack can be used.

FYI!

Vin Cox set a new record by biking around the whole world in just 176 days in 2010!

LONG-HAUL RIDING

For long-haul rides, you have to take more equipment: extra clothes, including clothing to wear in the evenings, and possibly a tent, sleeping bag and cooking gear. Some people use **panniers** to carry all their gear, but recently bike trailers have become increasingly popular. These usually fix on near the back wheel, and they can be used to carry a lot of equipment.

Get your **head** around the **headset**

The headset is the part of the bike that allows the handlebars to turn smoothly – so it's important that it works well at all times! Adjusting the headset, stem, **and** spacers **also allows you to change your riding position.**

No special tools are needed for this job.

REMOVE THE TOP CAP AND STEM

First, undo the top-cap bolt (this should come undone easily), then remove it and the top cap. Next, loosen the stem bolts on the side of the stem (these will be stiffer than the top cap because they have to be done up tightly). You should now be easily able to lift the stem and the spacers underneath it clear of the steerer. If not, the stem bolts may still be done up too tightly: loosen them a bit more, and try again.

FIND THE RIGHT RIDING POSITION

This is a good moment to see if you would prefer a lower or higher riding position. Try putting the stem under the spacers or some spacers under and some over the stem. If you want to climb on the bike and see how it feels, just tighten up the stem bolts to hold the stem temporarily in place. (Don't try to ride the bike like this, though!)

RETIGHTEN THE TOP CAP

Once you have found a position you like, screw the top cap back into place. Be careful: doing it up too tight will damage the headset. Once you feel a little resistance, screw the top-cap bolt in another quarter turn. This is the moment when you need to check that the handlebars are aligned (see page 37). Now tighten the stem bolts.

spacers sections of tube that fit onto a bike's steerer
steerer part of a bike's forks going through the frame and out at the top
stem part connecting the handlebars to the steerer

CHECK FOR TENSION

Grip the **steerer** in one hand, and pull on the front brake with the other while resting your stomach on the seat. Rock the bike back and forwards. If you can feel a slight knocking, the top cap is not done up tightly enough. Loosen the stem bolts, and tighten the top-cap bolt a quarter turn. Tighten the stem bolts, and check again until there is no knocking. Finally, lift the front of the bike up and twist the handlebars left and right several times. If they feel stiff, go back and loosen the top cap a quarter turn.

SECRET TRICK

If you make adjustments to the headset or stem, always double check that the stem is straight before tightening up the stem bolts:

1 Grip the front wheel between your knees, and line it up with the frame. You'll be able to see right away if the stem is straight (in this photo it isn't).

2 If not, grip the handlebars, and gently pull them around until the stem lines up perfectly (as in the photo below). Now you can tighten the stem bolts.

Changing handlebars

On any bike, changing the handlebars can make it feel like a different machine. You can get a higher, lower, wider or narrower riding position – on these pages we've shown a bike whose rider wanted a higher riding position. Add new grips or handlebar tape, and from the seat it starts to seem as if you're riding a whole new bike!

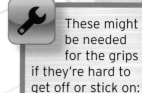

These might be needed for the grips if they're hard to get off or stick on:
- **Pot of water**
- **Screwdriver**
- **Sharp knife**
- **Hair gel**

Before and after: you can see how changing the handlebars will give this bike's rider a more upright riding position.

REMOVE GRIPS, LOOSEN BRAKE LEVERS AND SHIFTERS

First, take off the grips. Very rubbery ones will just roll back, like in the photo. If they won't do this, try lifting the edge with a screwdriver and getting a bit of water underneath them. This often frees things up. As a last resort, you may have to cut off the grips and replace them. Next loosen the allen bolts holding the brake levers and shifters in place. (On some bikes, especially road bikes, these are all contained in one unit.)

SECRET TRICK

Want your grips to hold solidly in place? Then you need some hair gel!

1 Put a little bit of gel on your fingertip, then rub it on the inside of the grip. Be careful not to use too much, because it takes days and days to dry.

TAKE OFF THE STEM PLATE

Undo the allen bolts holding the stem's front plate in place. The stem in the photo has four bolts, but many stems have only two. Be careful not to drop any of the bolts as the front plate comes off: they can be tricky to find again!

2 Slide the grip on to the handlebar. As long as you haven't used too much gel, the grips should be ready in a few hours.

FIX NEW BARS IN PLACE

Put grease on the place where the new bars will fit into the stem. Put them into place and re-fit the stem's front plate. Slide on the brake/ shifter levers, and fit the grips. Finally, tighten everything up fairly loosely, so that it's just possible to move things. Sit on the bike and get the handlebars at a comfortable position, then tighten the stem's front plate. Finally, adjust the angle of the brake levers and shifters to a comfortable position, and tighten them up.

grips rubbery tubes that fit over the handlebars to make them more comfortable for your hands
handlebar tape soft tape that is wrapped around road-bike handlebars to make them more comfortable

Become a pro mechanic

Most keen cyclists pick up a few mechanic's skills. But a few riders decide they want to earn their living working on bikes and become pro **mechanics.**

FYI!
On a pro bike-racing team, the mechanics are often first up in the morning, and last to bed at night.

STEP 1) BIKE SHOP

Most mechanics begin their professional career working in a bike shop. They have to do every job, from fixing flat tires to straightening frames that have been damaged in an accident. Most bike shops now send their mechanics on regular training courses to make sure their skills are up to date.

Emergency replacement of a derailleur during a 24-hour mountain-bike race.

STEP 2) RACE MECHANIC

If the shop a mechanic works for is associated with a racing team, he or she often gets involved in the race scene. At a race, you quickly find out if you can work under pressure: every second the riders lose because of a problem with their bike has to be won back.

off-season time when racing does not usually happen

pro short for professional, i.e. paid to do a skilled activity

directeur sportif French name for the head of a biking team, whose job is a bit like being a football coach

SECRET LIFE

Mechanics on a race team live a hard life during the racing season. Even before a race starts they work late into the night preparing the bikes.

In a big road race, team cars carrying spare bikes, wheels, and other supplies follow closely behind the riders.

Once the race is underway, one of the mechanics rides in the team car, ready to fix any problems.

This rider is getting advice from his *directeur sportif* **during a stage of the Tour de France. Also in the car is a team mechanic, ready to help if one of the team's bikes breaks.**

STEP 3) WORKING FOR A RACE TEAM

A few race mechanics get a reputation as calm, fast workers, who can prepare a bike quickly and repair any problem that comes up. They may get the opportunity to work for a race team full time. At the sport's top level, this means spending months away from home, living with the team during the race season. During the **off-season** the mechanic needs to live near the team headquarters, so that he or she can help develop next year's race bikes.

In a stage race, the other mechanics drive the team bus to the team's hotel. As soon as the riders arrive, they clean the bikes, change handlebar tape, and make any repairs that are needed.

Troubleshooting

Bicycles are very simple, and it's the same parts that get put under stress on all bikes. These are the parts that tend to break most often, and if there's something wrong with your bike they are likely to be the cause. Here are some of the most common problems, plus likely causes.

PROBLEM 1: SQUEAKING OR SQUEALING BRAKES
Rim brakes
• Check brake-pad alignment and adjust if necessary.
• Clean the rims and pads with fine sandpaper.
• Check the pads for small stones, bits of grit, etc., and pick out if necessary.
Disc brakes:
• Sand the rotors clean.
• Remove pads and check for wear and contamination with oil. If worn, replace; if contaminated, try baking them in a hot oven for half an hour. This sometimes cooks off the contaminant.

PROBLEM 2: TICKING NOISE FROM FRAME
Can be tricky to diagnose! First, make sure the noise isn't a shoelace or pants catching something on the bike every time you turn the pedals. Then try these:
• Undo and refasten wheel levers.
• Undo, grease and refasten **seatpost clamp**.
• Check that the seat clamp is done up tightly enough.
• Remove rear derailleur and, if present, rear **derailleur hanger**. Grease surfaces and threads, and refasten.
• Check that the headset and handlebar bolts are done up tightly enough.

PROBLEM 3: CLICKING OR CLACKING NOISE FROM BOTTOM BRACKET
It's very rare, but the bottom bracket or head tube areas of a bike can be damaged in a crash. First, check that the frame is not cracked.
• Check that crank bolts are done up tightly.
• Remove, clean, and reinstall cranks.
• Remove, clean, grease, and reinstall bottom bracket.
Noises that seem to come from the bottom bracket might actually be coming from elsewhere:
• Remove, grease and refit the seatpost.
• Undo, grease and refasten seatpost clamp.
• Undo and refasten wheel quick-release levers.

PROBLEM 4: GEARS WON'T SHIFT PROPERLY
This is almost always the gear cable stretching slightly, and has a simple solution:

• First adjust the gears using the barrel adjuster on the rear of the derailleur.
• Check that the rear derailleur, or the derailleur hanger, has not accidentally been bent. If it has, straighten it (it's best to ask a bike shop to do this for you because they will have a special tool). Sometimes on a carbon or aluminium frame, a detachable hanger has to be replaced rather than straightened.

buckle dent
derailleur hanger part to which the rear derailleur is bolted; on aluminium and carbon frames, it is usually a separate part; on steel frames, the derailleur bolts straight to the frame
seatpost clamp fastener that tightens to hold the seatpost at the correct height

PROBLEM 5: CHAIN KEEPS FALLING OFF

• Check that the rear derailleur, or the derailleur hanger, has not accidentally been

bent; if it has, take it to a bike shop for repair.
• Make adjustments to the limit screws (see page 21) on the front or rear derailleurs, depending on which cog the chain falls off.

PROBLEM 6: STEERING FEELS LOOSE OR WOBBLY

• Check tire pressure, especially on the front tire. If this is soft, it makes the steering feel very loose.
• Check that the handlebar-clamp bolts are done up tightly, and tighten if necessary.

PROBLEM 7: KNOCKING FEELING FROM HANDLEBARS WHEN BRAKING

• Make sure the front wheel's quick-release levers are done up tightly.
• Check the headset for slight movement; tighten if needed.

• Check that the brake pads are aligned and not worn down.
• Look at the wheel rims and see if they have a **buckle** anywhere.

SECRET TIP

One of the key skills for a mechanic is recognizing that there are some jobs you can't do. On modern bikes, some jobs require specialist tools that most people don't have at home:

Some wheels, for example, can't be taken apart and reassembled unless you have special tools like the one above.

The external-bearing bottom brackets fitted on the most expensive bikes also require special tools.

Jobs like these are usually best done by bike shops. With the right equipment, they will be able to do them quickly and without damaging your precious bike.

Glossary

balance bike small bike with no pedals used by young children

bearings short for 'ball bearings', tiny solid-metal balls that allow metal parts to move smoothly next to one another

bike pump hand powered pump for inflating bicycle tires

bloomers an early kind of trouser for women, baggy at the top and ending gathered at the knee

bottom bracket axle on a bicycle frame to which the cranks and pedals are attached

bottom bracket shell part of a bike's frame that holds the bottom bracket

breakable link special section of chain used to join two ends by hand

buckle dent

burr raised, uneven piece of metal

chainset the cranks and chainrings, which are linked to a bike's bottom bracket

coast to ride along on a bike without pedalling

cog toothed disc that fits into a bike's chain and grips it

cranks metal arms that join the pedals to the bike

derailleur hanger part to which the rear derailleur is bolted; on aluminium and carbon frames, it is usually a separate part; on steel frames, the derailleur bolts straight to the frame

derailleur hinged arm that moves the chain from side to side, allowing the bike to change gear

directeur sportif French name for the head of a biking team

drive side the side of the bike with the gears and chain on it (also sometimes called the right side)

drivetrain parts that let the rider power the bike along

fixing pin thin cylinder of metal designed to make joining two ends of a chain easier

flexibility how much and how easily someone can bend their joints

freewheel cluster of cogs attached to the bike's rear wheel

grips rubbery tubes that fit over the handlebars to make them more comfortable for your hands

handlebar tape soft tape that is wrapped around road-bike handlebars to make them more comfortable

jockey wheel small, toothed wheel inside the derailleur arm

knurl knob with a ridged surface, which makes it easier to grip

multi-tool bike tool with several different functions

off-season time when racing does not usually happen

panniers bags that are designed to hang down beside the wheel of a bicycle, attached to a rack

piston metal cylinder that slides in and out of its housing

pro short for professional, i.e. paid to do a skilled activity

rack framework on a bicycle to which luggage can be fastened

rigid frame a bike frame that does not have any kind of shock absorbers

seatpost clamp fastener that tightens to hold the seatpost at the correct height

seatpost tube that connects the seat to the bike frame

souplesse French word used to describe a smooth, rapid pedalling technique

spacers sections of tube that fit onto a bike's steerer

spindles outer parts of the bottom bracket, to which the cranks are bolted

square-taper bottom bracket most common type of bottom bracket

steerer the part of a bike's forks that goes up through the frame

stem the part of a bike that connects the handlebars to the steerer

third-hand tool special clamp used by mechanics to hold parts in place while they work on them

thread spiralling line cut into the length of a bolt or screw

valve part of an inner tube to which the pump attaches

Further information

REFERENCE BOOKS

There are several great books available for home bike mechanics.

Zinn and the Art of Road Bike Maintenance and *Zinn and the Art of Mountain Bike Maintenance* Lennard Zinn (Velo Press)

These have both been classic reference books for mechanics for years, and are regularly updated with new editions to keep up with changes in technology.

Passport to World Sports: BMX and Mountain Biking
Paul Mason (Capstone Press, 2011)

A great book for off-road enthusiasts, with descriptions of some of the world's best mountain-bike and BMX venues.

WEBSITES

FactHound offers a safe, fun way to find Internet sites related to this book. All of the sites on FactHound have been researched by our staff.

Here's all you do:

Visit ***www.facthound.com***

Type in this code: 9781429668828

45

Timeline

1817

Count Karl von Drais invents the *laufmaschine*, also known as the running machine, hobby horse, *Drasienne* and dandy horse. It is a pedal-less bicycle with a steerable front wheel.

1863

The Velocipede is developed, the first bike with pedals and a gear. It is so uncomfortable to ride that it becomes known as the Boneshaker.

1870

The 'ordinary' bicycle becomes popular, more often called the penny-farthing or high-wheeler. More comfortable than the Boneshaker, but far harder and more frightening to ride, the 'ordinary' is ridden mainly by brave young men.

1872

The first mass-produced ball-bearings become available – crucial because ball bearings allow two metal parts to rub smoothly against each other.

1879

In England, Henry J. Lawson invents a chain-driven bicycle called the Bicyclette.

1884

Thomas Stevens cycles from San Francisco to Boston in the USA, becoming the first person ever to cross North America by bike. It takes him three-and-a-half months. (By contrast, the Race Across America that is held every year takes about 10 days.) Stevens takes a rest, then goes on to cycle the rest of the way around the world, which takes him just over 2 years more.

1888

An Irish doctor named Dunlop fits an air-filled tire to his son's bicycle, aiming to give him a more comfortable ride.

1890

The 'safety cycle' appears, made of lightweight metal, with the rear wheel driven by pedals and a chain, and with two wheels the same size. This is the first recognizably modern bicycle. Because of the rough roads of the time, many of these safety cycles had front or rear suspension, or both.

1890s

Biking becomes increasingly popular – particularly among women. In 1894 Betty Bloomer invents the bloomer, which makes it possible for women to ride a bicycle. That same year, San Francisco sees the start of its first bicycle messenger service. In 1894-1895, Annie Kopchovsky (also called Annie Londonderry) becomes the first woman to cycle around the world.

1899

Marshall 'Major' Taylor becomes the world track biking champion at the one-mile distance. He is the second African-American to become world champion at any sport (the first was the Canadian boxer George Dixon).

1903

The Sturmey Archer Company in England develops a hub gear, which allows riders to choose different gears depending on the terrain they are covering. The hub-gear design would be common until the arrival of the derailleur in the 1950s.

1930
Italian bike-part designer Tulio Campagnolo invents the quick-release hub, the first of many innovative bicycle designs his company will develop.

1938
Simplex develops a simple cable-controlled rear derailleur. It does not work as well as today's parallelogram designs, and is not universally popular.

1950s
Tulio Campagnolo invents the cable-operated parallelogram derailleur. This major new design offers smooth, accurate shifting, and Campagnolo dominates the racing scene for the next 20-plus years.

1960s and 1970s
Biking becomes steadily more popular, first as a way of keeping fit, then as a way of saving fuel. The first Earth Day in 1970 begins a campaign of environmental awareness, and the Oil Crisis of 1973 makes fuel expensive and biking therefore more attractive.

1977
The first modern mountain bikes are developed by riders in the Marin County, California, area. Joe Breeze (Breezer) and Gary Fisher (Gary Fisher Bikes) are among those whose companies are still selling bikes today.

1984
Women's road racing appears at the Olympic Games for the first time. Bike gear numbers increase from 12 or 15 to 21 or 24. In the U.S., the Women's Mountain Bike And Tea Society is founded to encourage women to get out on mountain bikes.

1990s
Technological improvements include combined gear and brake levers, the first disc brakes for mountain bikes, and further increases in the number of gears available on bikes.

1996
Mountain biking appears at the Olympic Games for the first time.

2000s
High-end technology reaches amazing new levels, with 10-speed rear cogs allowing 20 or 30 gears on a bike, and Shimano introducing a digital gear-shifting system. Perhaps in response, some riders take the sport back to its roots, choosing single-speed and fixed-gear bikes. Many off-road races start to include special categories for single-speed riders.

Index